The Power of Positive Evangelism

The Power of Positive Evangelism

John R. Bisagno

BROADMAN PRESS
Nashville, Tennessee

© Copyright 1968 • BROADMAN PRESS
Nashville, Tennessee
All rights reserved
ISBN: 0-8054-2503-9
4225-03

DEWEY DECIMAL CLASSIFICATION NUMBER: 269.2
Library of Congress Catalog Card Number: 68-26918
Printed in the United States of America

CONTENTS

1

PREACHING

It is probably the height of presumption for one minister to suggest to another how to preach, and yet, within the framework of the modern-day revival, much can be learned by the sharing of ideas in the unique ministry of evangelistic preaching. Strange as it may seem, any preaching can be evangelistic if one creates a proper setting, finishes with an evangelistic appeal, and gives a good invitation.

One of the surprising things I discovered upon entering the pastorate was the ease with which the Holy Spirit blessed any type of preaching with evangelistic results when things were just right.

The first lesson came when the state executive secretary of our denomination, at my request, spoke to our people on the financial Cooperative Program. People had prayed, prospects were present, a warm situation was created, and seventeen additions to the church were recorded, nine of whom were by conversion and for baptism. Other settings of similar circumstances, with subjects preached not akin to an evangelistic theme, have produced conversions. Let us not lose sight of the fact that while evangelistic preaching is a unique art, little is more important than a warm service in which the power of the Holy Spirit is manifest.

Evangelistic preaching involves three things: (1) the preparation of the people and the preacher by much time alone with God; (2) the creation of a warm service—a genuine, friendly, happy setting created by the atmosphere of musician and preacher; and (3) the delivery of the sermon itself. Let the preacher be a man of prayer. Let him be cheerful and bright, creating a warm and friendly atmosphere, and an attitude that says, "I'll not crowd you now or in the invitation."

In short, a smile, an earnest delivery, and a genuine wholesome approach helps create an atmosphere of warmth that is imperative in the evangelistic service.

As for the preaching of the sermon, two factors are important: The first is delivery, the second, content. Sandy Koufax may earn as much as $100,000 a year for delivering a $3.95 baseball to the plate, while somewhere at the same time, a minor-league ballplayer is delivering a $3.95 baseball to the same plate for $5,000 a year. The difference is not in the baseball, it is in the delivery. Many of the world's great homilists simply do not deliver their payload well. The material is excellent; the delivery is poor.

Years ago, a pastor asked a famous actor why the great crowds came to see him act when he only acted out fiction. "I deliver the very oracles of God, and yet they do not come to hear me in droves. What is the difference?" Replied the actor, "You preach fact as though it were fiction and I preach fiction as though it were fact." Far too many of us preach the facts of the gospel as though they were fiction.

The old mountain preachers used to say when a man had finished a sermon, if he was not drippin' wet, walking on six inches of his britches leg, and so hoarse he couldn't speak above a whisper, that he had not preached at all.

While this might be an exaggeration, let it be remembered that fire in the pews and power down the aisle begins with fire in the pulpit. Let the pulpit blaze and the people will come to watch it burn.

If you find it difficult to put enthusiasm into the delivery of your message, remember that every sermon you preach may be your last. Lost men are dying. The devil is alive. Be enthusiastic. Throw every ounce of your body and soul into the delivery of every word. Let your eyes plead in love, scold in love, and reprove in love. Let your body vibrate with every ounce of passion in you, and preach as though it were your last sermon. What should men get more excited about than the love of God, the rebirth of the soul?

A large pulpit is not good. Pulpits should be small. Oral Roberts, one of the most effective preachers of our generation, never uses a pulpit. Many other successful ministers do the same. To be hidden behind a large pulpit robs the preacher of much of his effectiveness in the delivery of an evangelistic sermon. By all means, when preaching in a tent, stadium, or any large setting, use a lapel mike and be free to move.

If at all possible, preach without notes. Depend on the Holy Spirit to bring to mind the things you have studied and prepared. But, above all, prepare. Study your material. Read and reread. Get it off the paper into the brain and down into the heart, and preach from there. If notes are to be used, let them be no larger than the size of your Bible and placed between its leaves. Eye contact is important.

Look at your audience. Use gestures that are normal. Remember, there are several ways to get a point across.

One is by volume. Another effective way is to speak very softly, almost whispering into the microphone for a moment. Don't come on like Batman. Start low, go slow. Take fire, go higher. Use four or five seconds of silence after a profound statement. Speed up, slow down, be loud, be soft, change pace, use humor. Use good illustrations, but never quote names or places. Never use humor that may embarrass someone present. Never tell jokes about being overweight, cross-eyed, or buck-toothed. In every audience there is someone who will be offended! Use illustrations that are in good taste and above reproach. Make sure that your facts are correct. Don't feel that it is necessary to give credit to the source of your material. Remember, we are all throwing the same baseball and you can probably throw it better than the man who wrote it down in the book where you found it to begin with. Don't try to be Billy Graham or Hyman Appleman—be yourself. God has made you what you are to use you. There are people with whom you can communicate—people with whom you can be used of God that will be drawn to hear God's message through *you,* because God made you like you are and put you in their midst.

Don't preach too long in a revival, particularly in the week-night services. If you would increase your attendance and bring your crowds back night after night, close each service at a sensible hour. The people must travel home. They have children and must get up early in the morning for school and jobs.

Twenty-five or thirty minutes should be the maximum for a week-night evangelistic sermon. This, after a twenty-five or thirty-minute song service, will leave fifteen minutes for an invitation. You should be out one hour and fifteen or twenty minutes after you begin. Often the service can be done in an hour. Get the people in, stand up, say what you have to say, give an invitation, and go home.

Never use humor for humor's sake. Never use it just to get a laugh. Be sure that it is used to illustrate a point. Be sympathetic to your audience's needs. Don't become stereotyped. If humor is not in place in a particular situation, don't use it just because you always use it. Use good illustrations that will open the windows to let in the light of knowledge. Few people will remember anything you say in your sermons, but they will remember the illustrations.

As for suggested material, your own wisdom and the still small voice of the Holy Spirit will dictate the message needed for an hour. I would never announce six or eight sermons ahead of time. There may be reasons why you will need to change, and we must be sensitive to the Holy Spirit as to what we preach. Don't be adverse to changing at the last minute. Often you will have two or three sermons in mind until after the services have begun, and then decide on one on the platform. When you do change, don't apologize, just go ahead and preach.

There are certain subjects which must be dealt with in every revival—faith, God's love, heaven, hell, the joy of the Christian life, the need for repentance, and others. If you do not spend an entire sermon on each of them, by all means make much of them in some sermon. All of these should be referred to, if not preached on in an entire message, during the course of a revival.

Personally, I feel that there are at least two subjects that must be dealt with at length in every revival. One is the need for the new birth and the explanation of it, and the other is the second coming of Christ. I know of no subjects more important than these.

After twelve years in the evangelistic field, I feel that I could sum up the eight themes with which I most consistently dealt, in the following list:

1. The Need for Revival
2. The New Birth
3. The Love of God
4. Repentance
5. Childhood Conversion
6. Calvary
7. The Dedication of Teen-agers
8. The Second Coming of Christ

To some degree or other, present all of these important doctrines with clarity and power in every evangelistic situation.

A personal word: I have found no message over the years that God has consistently blessed as the message on the second coming of Christ. Eddie Martin, Hyman Appleman, Jack Shuler, Billy Graham, and other evangelists have made that same statement.

2
INVITATION

There have been revivals in which some of the out-standing preachers in the world have preached to overflow audiences, night after night, with only two or three conversions. I have seen ministries in which mediocre preachers have consistently had fifty to one hundred conversions week after week. The difference? The power of the Holy Spirit, yes; preparation, yes; the power of God, yes; but I believe that the big physical difference is that all-important phase of the Christian ministry—*the ability to give an invitation.* It is a God-given gift and one that will not be learned overnight, and yet, as in most things, there are some rules to be learned. There are basic mistakes often made, which if corrected, can produce consistent results. I know of no other phase in the entire ministry of the preacher more important than drawing the net. Yet, it is at this point that most of us fail. No college or seminary courses are offered, few sermons ever preached on how to give an invitation, yet it is here that we win or lose it all. The invitation is hard.

Extending an invitation is the greatest agony in the ministry. We live and die a thousand deaths in the ten or twenty minutes in which the invitation is extended. When souls stand between life and death, we must be most de-

13

pendent upon the Holy Spirit and most sensitive to his leadership. An invitation extended too long may harden some heart that can never again be touched. An invitation prematurely closed may miss that one last soul that was going to come on the next verse. Which of us feels competent to write instructions to our fellow ministers on the giving of an invitation?

I feel like the man who was dying and called a doctor. After three hours of X rays and examination, the doctor said, "I am afraid you are going to die. Are there any last words?" "Yes," the man said, "I wish I had called another doctor."

I do not presume to tell you how to give an invitation. This must be learned in the laboratory of experience and in the school of prayer, yet there are some constant factors that should be remembered. Following are twelve suggestions that have been helpful in my own ministry at the point of extending the invitation.

1. *Give the invitation authoritatively.*—A note of authority, or the lack of it, is one of the keys to a successful ministry and one of our worst failures in giving the invitation. Set your invitation on fire and people will come and watch the fire burn. A fire must itself burn before it can give warmth to others. If *you* don't believe it, they won't believe it. Stand up on your hind legs and give the invitation with all the authority of heaven. Your frame of mind, your attitude, your approach to it all is of utmost importance. If you approach the invitation hesitantly, with a note of apology, you might as well not give it at all. Don't hesitate. Don't apologize for it—just give it! The preacher's atti-

tude is extremely important and the man in the pew can read your attitude. You have the authority of heaven behind you. Demand repentance, decisions, and action.

One reason we lack authority in the invitation is that we have so often heard criticism of high-pressure invitations that we go into the invitation whipped—afraid of criticism from someone. What is high pressure? I have heard a lot about it, but in fifteen years in the ministry, I have never seen any high pressure. I have never heard an evangelist tell a deathbed story; I have never heard a tearjerker. I am convinced that in most cases high pressure simply means that someone else is getting the job done. If you would avoid criticism, say nothing, do nothing, and be nothing. He that would seek accomplishments and success in winning men to Christ must run the risk of the criticism of those who do nothing.

It has come to the sad state that many churches do not even give invitations anymore. May God have mercy on us. Forget what people think! You must have an authority about your ministry, especially in extending invitations, or men will not respond.

2. *Be specific.*—Never assume that your audience knows what you want them to do. A great number do not.

Several years ago a famous preacher preached an inspiring sermon on "doing something." The next day fifty men responded to the challenge, excitedly asking for something to do. The preacher confessed that he did not have anything special in mind. The fifty laymen bound themselves together to place a Bible in every hotel room in the world, and the Gideons were born.

Frequently we ask from the pulpit, Who will come for baptism, Who will come on conversion? Who will come by statement, letter, special service? The average man in the pew doesn't know letter from better, or position from profession. We must spell out exactly what it is we are asking them to do.

Some years ago an evangelist was holding a revival in Oklahoma. After three nights of preaching on communism without any kind of visible results, he moaned to the educational director, "I cannot understand why they are not coming forward." "What do you want them to do?" asked the educational director. "Come down and surrender to join the FBI?"

Explain step by step that if they are willing to change their way of life, confess their sin, put Christ as Lord and Master of their life, you want them to step out in the aisle. Explain how simple it is if they will take that first step, then the second, then the third and come to the front.

3. *Give it urgently.*—Never ask them to think it over. Never talk about tomorrow. Never refer to another chance. Jesus always called for action *today.* Immediately, tonight, on this verse, in this service, it is always now! now! now!

4. *Get into the invitation.*—The careless, unplanned manner in which many ministers and musicians make the transition from song service to message of invitation is one of the reasons for the failure of many invitations. Too often the invitation is thought of as unimportant, something to be tacked on to the end of the sermon. If you want to kill the service and the invitation, preach a splendid thirty-minute sermon, end on high with a thrilling illustration, and

then kill it all by saying, "We shall stand and sing three verses of hymn number so-and-so, whether anyone comes or not!" Never infer that people might not come. Never be negative in an invitation. Get into the invitation without anyone's knowing it. A sharp break between sermon and invitation can destroy it all. An invitation number should never be announced. It should only be sung, softly in the background, as the invitation is extended. If you want to kill the service, finish your sermon by turning to the song leader and saying, "What is the invitation number?" You might just as well go home right there. You have lost the battle.

After the people have been looking in the evangelist's face for thirty minutes, they should immediately close their eyes and let the next image be a picture of God as they envision him. Their thought should be immediately turned to their relationship with the Lord. If, between the message and the hymn, they look at a songbook or song leader, they will be distracted.

They should never look from the face of the preacher to a page in the songbook and then close their eyes and look to God. Books should not be used by the audience in the invitation at all, except in rare instances toward the end of the invitation.

When the preacher has finished preaching, have the organist and choir primed to come in softly, humming or playing, during the last seconds of his closing illustration. This should be done by a prearranged signal from the musician. There should be no movement of any kind by the song leader on the platform until all heads are bowed.

Another possibility is that at the end of the message, the evangelist will bow his head and start praying, or he may say, "As we all bow our heads," and then keep on talking as he moves into the invitation. Or, he may or may not pray between the message and the invitation. But he should move as quickly, as smoothly, as unnoticeably as possible, from the message to having them bow their heads while the choir sings.

The opening verses should be sung only by the choir. It is nice to use a soloist occasionally on the invitation, but only toward the end of an invitation as a closing appeal.

The loud playing of the piano at the beginning of an invitation, when a smooth transition is being made, can be distracting. The opening strains of the invitation music, as the choir softly comes up in the background, should be accompanied only by the organist. It is only as the pace increases and the congregation joins in with the invitation that the piano should play. If only a piano is available, let its notes be slow and soft.

The song leader should never move his hands in the direction of the audience during an invitation. This is distracting to the audience, whose attention should be only on the minister. If the choir leader directs the choir during the invitation, let him do so with his back to the audience with gestures small and unnoticeable, standing directly in back of the evangelist. If, however, the evangelist asks the audience to sing, he should then step back, making himself almost a part of the choir, and lead the audience only with his voice. Hand directing should never be used with the audience during the invitation.

The minister and musicians should have a predetermined understanding as to who will change the invitational hymn. If the minister desires the song leader to change the song during the invitation, he should inform him ahead of time. However, because it is the evangelist who is in charge of extending the invitation, it is my opinion that he is the one that should make the changes as the invitation continues. This may be done in one of two ways. As heads are bowed, he can whisper softly to the song leader to change the invitation number. Or, the evangelist may say to the congregation, using the theme of the next hymn in his invitation, "Now as the choir begins to sing 'Almost Persuaded now to Believe,' why don't you who are almost persuaded come and make your decision tonight?" If the song leader is informed ahead of time, he can have the music ready.

It is often good, when the invitation begins to drag, for the evangelist to signal for a final two or three verses by asking everyone to stand and sing, "I Am Resolved" or "Stand Up, Stand Up for Jesus," or other militant numbers.

It would be wise for the organist, pianist, and song leader to have a list of ten invitation numbers, numbered from one to ten, so that during the invitation as the hymn is changed, the evangelist can raise up three fingers for "Just As I Am" or four for "Almost Persuaded Now to Believe," and so on. The opening invitation hymn should be the same every night and should be a hymn that is familiar. Also, it should be one that is predetermined by the evangelist and the song leader before the services begin. It should be obvious that an invitation is no place to introduce new music.

5. *Give the invitation positively.*—Never say, "If you are going to come," but, "Since you are going to come." Never say, "Will you come," but, "As you come." Never plant a negative thought. Always assume that they will come and that you expect them to come and all things are in readiness. You can help plant a positive thought in their minds. "Now you know you are going to come, you want to come, you have planned to come and now, as you do come, come quickly." It is often wise to say, "I'll meet you at the front," or, "I am leaving the platform; you leave as I do and meet me here at the altar." As they do come, take a few steps down the aisle toward them with a smile on your face, greeting them as they come. Tell them that you would be glad to come back and walk with them. Go to any length to help them to come. It is often good to say, "Make up your mind while you are still seated that you are going to come." "You came tonight because you were interested, you want to make a decision—so don't hesitate, don't delay by waiting two or three verses, but as you stand, just keep right on moving and we will meet you at the front."

Bo Baker for years has used the positive approach of urging them to stand and come forward all in one motion, saying, "You know you are going to come; as you do, we will wait for you."

In the event that no one responds to the invitation, never scold the audience. Instead, thank God that they were there and tell the people how good it has been to be present and what a wonderful service we are going to have tomorrow night. Dismiss them on an optimistic note. Leave the service on high. Never bawl out the audience at the end of an invitation, else the next night the crowd will be down 50 percent.

6. *Give the invitation prayerfully.*—Of course, the invitation is to be bathed in great prayer. I have found in my own ministry that there is a direct relationship between the number of people who have come down the aisle and the amount of time I have spent in prayer over that particular service. Power makes people come forward in the invitation. No prayer, no power. Little prayer, little power. Much prayer, much power.

As you extend the invitation, let your heart keep talking to God. As you speak, affirm in your heart, "I believe the Holy Spirit is working. I know, dear God, that you are dealing with hearts. I believe more will come forward tonight." Pray in great faith. Expect things to happen and God will honor your faith.

7. *Give it proudly.*—In your preparation for the service, including music and preaching, plan for the invitation itself. Remember that as a representative of the King of kings, it is your holy position to extend the offer of grace to lost and dying men. It is an honor to be called from among the ranks of men to the ministry of the gospel as colaborers with Christ. Throw your shoulders back, look discerningly into the faces of the people, and urge them to receive Jesus Christ.

Make everything in the invitation the very best. Often the musicians will tend to let down. Have the choir stand proudly to their feet, look into the eyes of the conductor, and harmonize more beautifully than ever while singing the invitation hymn. Too often we carefully rehearse the special music and give little thought to the performance of the invitational hymn. Many times, Cliff Barrows will rehearse Billy Graham's crusade choirs for an hour and a half before the opening night of the crusade on "Just As I Am." Rehearse the hymn of invitation. Go over every detail of the invitation in your mind and execute it to the best of your ability.

Years ago, the first transoceanic cable message came from the king of England to the waiting hearts of millions of Americans. Seconds before the broadcast, the engineer discovered that the cable had been broken. Dramatically grasping both ends of the cable in his hands, for twenty-seven minutes the message of the king flowed through his body to the nation. In just that way, every time we stand to give an invitation, we allow ourselves to be channels through which the Spirit of Christ flows into the hearts of waiting sinners. It is a privilege to extend the invitation of the King of kings—do it proudly!

8. *Don't be afraid to give a long invitation.*—It is thrilling to see the heavens open and a flood of power come as great hosts respond on the first word of the invitation. However, it is usually true that little or no response will occur immediately and a good deal of time is often required for an invitation. While we realize that God speaks to sinners as we preach, it is often easier for him to speak in the quietness of the invitation as we step back and let him move.

When we go into an invitation with plans to sing only two or three verses, we are saying that what we have said for thirty minutes is more important than what God may say in a minute and a half. *I have found that 90 percent of the converts come forward after the third verse of the invitation.* On a recent Sunday morning in our church, we sang nine verses without a move. This was highly unusual, but I was impressed that many were on the verge of decision. When the invitation finished, twenty-five minutes later, twenty-seven had been converted, including nine grown men.

In extending a long invitation, some variety is needed. After the invitation begins, it is often wise not to speak for three or four verses. When things begin to slow, several things can be done to keep the invitation from dragging.

(1) People may be seated and then stand again.

(2) Ask the folks to step back, that those in the middle may move to the aisle more easily.

(3) Ask Christians to speak a word of encouragement to a friend or loved one standing nearby. No one will ever be offended by a simple, "I'll go with you."

(4) Ask them to look up at you while you speak a word of encouragement and then to bow their heads again.

(5) Stop and reemphasize some point or use an illustration. In other words, let them look up at you, preach another minute or two, and then go on with the invitation.

(6) Encourage Christians to come forward and pray for friends, rededicate their lives, or join the church. Their coming may break the ice and make it easy for the unconverted to respond.

(7) Change the invitational hymn. Use a soloist for part of the invitation as you approach its conclusion. If the Holy Spirit is moving in great power and variety is used, a long invitation will not be distasteful and will prove to be very fruitful.

9. *Give a good rededication invitation.*—Never minimize the importance of rededication. Many times a rededication of life actually means more in changing the direction and purpose of a person's life than his conversion. Be specific in the rededication invitation. Spell it out.

A rededication should mean more than "I will try harder," or "I just want a closer walk with the Lord." It should mean one of two things: (1) "There are some definite things I am doing that are wrong, and I intend to stop immediately," or (2) "There are some definite things I am not doing—such as tithing, studying the Bible, witnessing, praying, attending church, and so on—that I intend to start immediately." It is that simple. In short, a rededication means that in every area of a person's life, Christ is to be given first place henceforth.

10. *Deal properly with those who come.*—Whether a person comes to join the church, be converted, or rededicate his life, the pastor or some counselor should pray with him and lead him to pray, to confess his sins to God, to dedicate his influence anew, or whatever the need may be. I have dealt with many teen-agers and adults who went forward, saying that they had made decisions as children, but did not know what they were doing. In most cases I have found that they really did know what they were doing, but that the individual who dealt with them did not know

what *he* was doing. What a tragic mistake to merely shake hands with the person, then have him fill out a card and be seated. Humble yourself, get on your knees, and deal properly with those who come, and a far greater quality of decisions will be made. By all means, don't give them a card to sign until they have prayed and their decision has been made. Do not give the card first. You may interfere with the Holy Spirit's dealing with them. Lead them quickly into their decision for Christ. The information can be recorded later.

11. *Make much of their decision.*—Too often we merely read the names of those who come: "So-and-so comes on profession of faith." "So-and-so comes on rededication." Say something about each one. Let some of them give a testimony. Shake their hands and congratulate them on their decision. Ask friends, Sunday School teachers, or parents to come and stand by them. Let them know that we believe this is a genuine experience in their life. It is a mistake to ask the church clerk to read off the names and tell the decision. There is no warmth in that. The church clerk probably has not led them to Christ.

Let the pastor, as shepherd of the people, present those who come, and speak a word about their decision.

Sunday by Sunday, consistently encourage the people to come by and greet those who have made decisions at the front. When 95 percent of the people head for the back door, it is like saying to the new convert: "We didn't really care whether you came or not, we were just saying that." Take time to make much of the invitation, and even more of those who have responded to it.

3

MUSIC

In 1955, I received a Bachelor of Music degree under the renowned Dean Angell at Oklahoma Baptist University. In addition to being a preacher, I am proud to have been an evangelistic musician for over seven years. I cannot say enough about the importance of a good, warmhearted evangelistic song service and its contribution to the success of a revival. How heartily do I agree with the statement made to me by Dr. T. B. Lackey several years ago: "John, a good song service is half the battle any day." While it is by the foolishness of preaching that God has chosen to win the lost, I have seen many occasions in which people were converted when an invitation was given after a concert of sacred music. The difference between preaching and singing the message of the Lord is that in music it is done on predetermined pitches. Never underrate the power of a well-planned, warmhearted song service. It is, indeed, half the battle any day!

Let it be remembered that the preacher and singer are a team, praying, planning, producing together. And yet, as any effective team must have a quarterback, the preacher is the leader of the entire evangelistic team. He is always to be in charge of the planning and executing of the evangelistic services from beginning to end, from the opening choir number to the last amen. It is he who is responsible for the overall success of the finished product. I have found that the dedicated musician would have it no other way. Let the preacher remember, however, that this place of respect and leadership must be earned, not demanded.

The first step in planning a good music program is the selection of the singer. This is the responsibility of the church pastor or the crusade chairman and should be prayerfully considered months in advance. The man you seek is no ordinary man. He is not necessarily equipped simply because he is a talented soloist, composer, or piano teacher. The ability to feel out the heartstrings of a revival congregation, to be sympathetic to the mood and needs of a crowd of people, is a rare and priceless gift. It can only come by an awareness of the voice of the Holy Spirit as the revival singer responds to the spiritual ebb and flow of the moment. Pity the poor singer who tries the "youth for Christ" style with a convocation of old ladies, or who would be a Cliff Barrows in a country church. The stereotyped, one-gear musician will hardly be at home on the revival platform.

Above all, the singer must be in empathy with what is being done. Eggs are not hatched in a refrigerator but in an incubator. Spiritual rebirths in the hearts of men will seldom take place in a cold service. It is the singer's primary responsibility to create a relaxed, happy, informal, spiritual atmosphere in which the man in the pew will not feel that he is doing something completely out of place to come weeping his way to the altar.

The evening evangelistic service is not a duplication of the formal Sunday morning service. Everything is different. The pace is quicker, the atmosphere more relaxed. The entire setting from prelude to benediction must be geared in a different mood. Everything is directed toward creating an atmosphere in which the man in the pew can come forward with ease. Unless the entire program points to a fruitful invitation, the aiming is wrong. When we lose there, we lose it all, and the service begins with the opening notes of the organ prelude.

After the singer has been selected, he should immediately write to the pastor and music director and commence plans for the meeting. Care should be given to securing accompanists who are experienced, adept at, and in sympathy with evangelistic music. A Bach chorale for the offertory, "A Mighty Fortress Is Our God" for an opening hymn, certainly constitute some of the world's great music, but both are out of place in a revival song service. A long-haired musician at the piano or organ, frowning and scowling during rehearsal, song service, and invitation, will break the spirit of the singer and preacher alike and should never be tolerated.

You may be assured that the audience is sensitive at this point and that any friction between team members is obvious to them. Be careful in the selection of capable, empathic accompanists.

The choir, likewise, should be in complete accord in their desire to assist the congregation in the song service. Robes may or may not be worn. In my opinion, dark skirts and slacks with white blouses and shirts help to create a greater air of informality, and yet lend grace and uniformity to the appearance and presentation of the music during week-night services.

At least a month before the revival begins, a giant revival choir attendance poster should be displayed in the lobby of the church. Using the adult choir as a nucleus in the sign-up campaign, add youth choirs and volunteers for a great revival choir. Add extra chairs to the platform. Let them spill over to the floor below, if necessary, but by all means have a large choir. A big choir has an exciting effect on the people. It says to them, this is important, this is unusual, this is special. That kind of excitement is contagious.

A choir loft packed nightly will help to assure a packed auditorium. People like to go where the action is. Give it to them in a dynamic, exciting, overflow choir and a thrilling evangelistic song service—and watch them come!

The choir can be of great value in salvaging the Saturday night services as well. Don't give up on Saturday. From the word go, begin promoting a big musical concert for Saturday, with special requests, favorites, and specials. Challenge the choir from the opening night to help make Saturday night a great success by being present. Choir attendance can be promoted by dividing the choir into teams such as the "sharps" and "flats," or the "chords" and "dis-chords." Keep an attendance count every night. Plan a big choir fellowship at the conclusion of the Saturday night services with the losers entertaining the winners in a social hour.

Before the revival begins, designate meeting places with

the musicians, and urge upon all involved the importance of staying on schedule. A good schedule might be:

6:30 P.M.—Meet with accompanist to outline detailed order of services for all concerned. This would include selection of prelude numbers for both organist and pianist; understanding of introductions, tempos, and the like. It is then that questions can be worked out, such as, "Will sharps be transposed to flats?" "Which portion of which hymn will be used as an introduction?" "What about modulation?"

6:45 P.M.—Soloists and all special groups such as trios and quartets should be present. They should be informed where to be seated, that they might move as quickly as possible to the pulpit. If someone other than the regular accompanist is to accompany any special soloist or groups, seat them next to the piano and not in the audience, enabling them to move quickly to the piano bench.

7:00 P.M.—Rehearse the revival choir. Do not hesitate to rehearse the choir in the auditorium in front of the audience. Many people like to come early to hear the choir practice. Promptness should be emphasized to choir members. Remind them that a five-minute-late start may make the failure rather than the success of some number, or a delay in starting the services. A service advertised to start at seven-thirty should not begin at seven thirty-five. A good revival song leader can work up a choir special in twenty minutes.

7:20 P.M.—The choir should be dismissed to relax and get a drink, then line up outside the loft ready to march in precisely at seven-thirty after a word of prayer.

7:25 P.M.—The prelude should begin no later than five minutes before service time. The most desirable prelude and song services are played by organ and piano. If an organ is not available, move in a second piano and use two. Check on intonation before the revival begins. An organ alone should not be used, but a piano should always join with the organ to help put the heart of the tempo into the music. The prelude should consist of two verses each of two or three slow numbers, such as "There Is a Fountain," "The Old Rugged Cross," or "What a Friend We Have in Jesus," followed by two or three fast numbers, such as "Stand Up, Stand Up for Jesus," "Power in the Blood," or "When We All Get to Heaven." The prelude leads up to an introduction presentation at seven-thirty as the choir enters. These numbers should be determined ahead of time at the six-thirty rehearsal and played by both accompanists.

Promptly at seven-thirty, they should begin playing the predetermined revival theme with which the choir opens the services every night. Something like "Breathe on Me" or "Sweet Hour of Prayer" is not a good revival theme. The number should be bright, fast, and enthusiastic, one that will make the choir want to march in smiling and make the people want to stand up and sing.

Again, be certain to start the services promptly at seven-thirty on a bright, cheerful, militant note. Nothing slow and prayerful should be used to open an evangelistic service. You can always slow down the pace of an exciting service, but it is difficult to build after a slow beginning.

As the last five or six members of the choir are taking their places, the song leader will walk from the side room to the pulpit, followed by the pastor, or chairman, and the evangelist. As the choir remains standing and the ministers are seated, the song leader will walk in and face the choir and begin directing the choir theme. The first sound from the platform after the organ and piano prelude should not be that of the singer or the pastor addressing the audience, but that of the choir singing. Let them announce the opening of services with the presentation of the theme.

A good outline for the service itself could be as follows:

7:30—Opening choir number
7:31—First congregational hymn
7:34—Prayer chorus
7:35—Prayer
7:36—Special number by ensemble, song leader, or choir
7:38—Second hymn
7:41—Announcements by pastor and recognition of visitors
7:45—Testimonies, led by song leader or evangelist
7:48—Last hymn
7:50—Offering
7:55—Second special number by ensemble, choir, or song leader
8:00—Sermon
8:25—Invitation
8:40—Presentation of new members
8:45—Benediction

One hour and fifteen minutes is ample time for a weeknight revival service, except where a tremendous breakthrough in the invitation is experienced. An extended service taking one and one-half to two hours should not be because the song service or the sermon is longer than usual, but because the Holy Spirit has nightly moved in the invitation and extended it. Most of the time, the entire service can be closed in an hour and fifteen minutes.

Closing the service on time will help to assure a return crowd the following night. If day services are held, the music should be kept at a minimum, including not over two hymns and a special number, not to exceed fifteen minutes. At these morning services, the messages are generally of a teaching nature and will take longer.

As the song service actually begins with the opening choir number, the singer will immediately turn to the audience and begin the services. Several factors should be remembered.

1. With the exception of some of the grand hymns, such as "All Hail the Power of Jesus' Name," "Love Divine, All Loves Excelling," and "Come, Thou Almighty King," a good vibrato should be used by the organist. Although I know many musicians do not like to use the vibrato and will disagree, it is my opinion that the vibrato adds a great deal of needed warmth to an evangelistic song service. The average evangelistic numbers—such as "I Am Resolved," "Love Lifted Me," and "Oh, How I Love Jesus"—should not be played without a vibrato. There is a lilt, a warmth, in the vibrato that is helpful in the creation of a warm atmosphere in a revival song service.

2. The congregation should always stand on the first song. As the service begins and the opening number is announced, let the song leader make an upward gesture with his hand, indicating that people are to rise.

3. The organist should then play the first and last two measures of the hymn as an introduction. It should be understood, ahead of time, which accompanist is to play the introduction. It should be loud and clear and end on the tonic chord.

4. The opening song should not be in a multiple rhythm, such as 6/8 or 12/8. A compound rhythm can too easily be dragged by accompanist and congregation. Let the opening hymn be one with a good, solid, tempo, such as "Revive Us Again" in 3/4, or "Stand Up, Stand Up for Jesus," "Onward, Christian Soldiers," or "Down at the Cross," in 4/4.

5. Never go from a fast introductory number immediately into a prayer. The bright opening number should be followed by a warm, melting number, such as "Breathe on Me," "Thank You, Lord," or "Must Jesus Bear the Cross Alone."

After the spirit of the congregation has settled and while the people are still standing, ask them to sing it softly once again with heads bowed, and remain with heads bowed as the pastor comes to pray. During the prayer, it is often nice for the choir to hum softly in the background. A word of caution, however. Creating this beautiful atmosphere may cause the preacher to become inspired and pray for five minutes. If this happens, let the choir stop humming after the first two verses. Long prayers are as out of place in a revival service as long sermons.

6. After the first prayer, it is usually not necessary for the pastor or song leader to ask the people to be seated. When the pastor is seated, this will normally be the signal

for the congregation to do likewise. If not, a slight downward movement of the hand by the song leader should be sufficient.

7. As the audience is being seated, let the accompanist immediately begin the introduction of the first special.

8. The brighter, faster numbers should be used here with the slow, quieting numbers to precede the message. Except in rare cases where the evangelist will request a change to help create a particular effect, the number immediately preceding the sermon should be a slow, moving number, rather than a rousing, militant one. Remember that the directing of an evangelistic song service is an art and a ministry in itself. The evangelistic artist should be as fluid as possible and as sensitive to the people and leadership of the Holy Spirit as he can be.

9. A common problem of an inexperienced director is allowing the accompanist to rush or drag the tempo. A good, firm beat, with a commanding pattern and a note of authority in voice and appearance will always keep you as song leader in control of the situation. Don't let the accompanist lead you. Be sure that you lead him.

10. Don't be afraid to use a big pattern, but don't overdo it, particularly if the audience is small. The congregation is not just another choir that you can direct with a simple flick of the wrist or movement of the hand. While you will not want to look like a windmill in a tornado, you will want to put all of your personality and ability into the enthusiastic directing of the people. *Mere announcing of hymns and beating of patterns does not inspire people to sing.*

11. An encouraging word, a brief explanation—all are in place when done quickly but not overdone by the revival singer.

12. Never snap your fingers.

13. Don't talk too much.

14. Don't tell stories between verses.

15. If the service is tense, the audience unresponsive, don't be afraid to inject a small note of humor.

16. Above all, be sensitive to the need of the moment and work toward the molding of a thrilling atmosphere that points to the sermon and invitation, when men will be convinced through song and sermon to respond to the Saviour.

17. A word of caution about special music. When outside specials are used, they should be by people who are in sympathy with what you are trying to do. Such people should never attend the revival and leave after their number is performed. When specials are presented by members of the local congregation, they should be people who are a faithful part of the revival choir. Careful attention should be given to the selection of the special music. The song leader should always ask what the soloist or ensemble intends to sing. He may then ask them to change if the choice is not in keeping with good revival music.

Three common mistakes are made in the selection of revival music. First is the use of a number that is good music, but better for Sunday morning than for a revival song service. Such numbers might include "I Walked Today Where Jesus Walked" and "The Holy City." Second, avoid the selection of a number that seems to be a religious number, but whose theology is weak, such as "I Believe" and

"He." A careful analysis will show that they have little theology or erroneous theology. These are beautiful popular numbers and have a place, but certainly not in a revival. Revival is the time to sing of the joy of the Christian life, the love of God, the need for repentance, the urgency of salvation.

There is a third kind of song that is completely removed from the evangelistic situation but that is sometimes used in revivals. Such numbers are "Trees," "God Bless America," and believe it or not, I have even heard "Old Black Joe" used in revivals.

Let the revival musicians join daily with all members of the revival team in prayer for the leadership and power of the Holy Spirit. Sing songs that exalt Jesus. Keep a bright smile on your face. Fill the services with joy and expectancy. Always be in command of the situation. Look straight into the eyes of the people. Don't talk too much, always leave them wanting more, and you will go a long way in contributing to the greatest task in the world—the building of an evangelistic service in which men are won to Christ. (See the chapter on "Invitation" for more information pertinent to revival music.)

4

THE OFFERING

Attitude! Remember that word. In the final analysis, the success of the offering depends upon the attitude of the one who takes it.

After spending over twelve years in the evangelistic field and watching hundreds of men take offerings, it seems that the most important factor is this: Does the pastor really want a visiting evangelist to get a good offering? If he does, he can get it. I know many pastors and full-time evangelists who consistently conduct revivals. I believe that I speak authoritatively when I say I do not know a man who would not be satisfied with the offering that the people gave, whether large or small, if the pastor did all he could to take it. If he genuinely wants to get a good offering and seeks it in a positive way, with some preparations outlined herein, a good offering will be assured. But if he fails in some of the simple mechanics of taking a good offering and does not really want the man to have a good offering, the people will recognize it and will not respond.

In inviting a visiting preacher to conduct a revival, the pastor should consider several things. If the church is small and unable to give sizable offerings, an outside singer should not be employed. A 60-40 percent division of the offering will not mean a worthy amount for either of God's servants in the event the offering is small. In this case it is best to use a local man to do the music, with the understanding that he will be given an honorarium from the budget.

By all means, it should be clearly understood in advance who is going to get what. It is both dishonest and impractical to receive a love offering in the name of the evangelist and give part to the building fund or church treasury, if this was not clearly stated night by night as the offering was received.

Is an honorarium to be given to the organist and pianist? If so, it should be arranged for in a business meeting or in the planning of the annual church budget, but clearly defined and agreed upon *ahead of time.* It should not be taken from the love offering for the visiting preacher.

One of the most common mistakes made in receiving love offerings, or any type of offering for that matter, is to presume that we must protect the people's pocketbook by not trying very hard. If you make up your mind to get a good offering, one that will be a true expression of love and a blessing to the recipient, then ask for it positively, prayerfully, and with great anticipation. The people will protect their own pocketbooks.

If you do it negatively, the people, the evangelist, and the Lord will be embarrassed. I have seen men take offerings when it was obvious that they really weren't trying and didn't care how much the love offering was. They always hand it to the evangelist and say, "My, we are sorry it couldn't have been more." They really weren't sorry at all. They didn't want it to be more or they would have tried.

Perhaps they were afraid of their people or were afraid they would give too much and hurt the church budget, but remember, you cannot outgive God. You do your people a great service when you lead them to give liberally and let them know you expect them to do so. The Lord will bless your church as you bless the men of God who preach from your pulpit. Our people will not give more than they can. Let them worry about that; you need not protect them.

Love offerings that are a guaranteed amount in the budget are no love offerings at all. I, personally, would rather receive $200 that was a genuine expression of the love of the people who gave all they could, than $300 that was a "fee" paid to hire a preacher for the week.

When you discuss the forthcoming revival with your evangelist, discuss the manner of the receiving and dividing of the love offering frankly. Don't embarrass him by expecting him to bring up the subject. Tell him your church's usual policy and ask him his desires. When you accepted the call to the pastorate of the church, you probably discussed the salary with the pulpit committee. You should do the same with the men you invite. This is good sense and good business. Don't pretend that it isn't important and that just anything will do. It *is* important and just anything *won't* do. The care of our family, education of our children, and payment of our bills are important to all of us. Have a clear understanding and do the best you can in the offering. I have never had to apologize for an offering I gave a man, or for any cause. It is with a great deal of pride that I hand a good-sized offering check to every man that preaches from my pulpit. God blesses a cheerful giver.

He likewise blesses a church that expects to do big in the matter of the love offering.

If you lead your people to think negatively and to give small, the chickens will come home to roost in your whole ministry and church. God must make big men for the big places. Part of our Christian "bigness" is our genuine desire to share. Make up your mind whether you *really* want this man to have a good offering. If you do, let your people know it, and they will never give an offering that you will be embarrassed to hand to a visiting preacher.

How much offering is enough for a visiting evangelist? In answering this, many factors should be considered. For denominational workers, pastors, and missionaries who have a steady income from other sources, it is obvious that less is required than for the full-time evangelist with no other means of livelihood. Whether the man is the pastor of a large church with a large income or not, I know of none of God's men that are overpaid. Men with big incomes and big churches usually have big expenses. Most $15,000- to $20,000-a-year men could be making $100,000 a year if their talents were dedicated to the business world. You do not need to protect the people from giving too much, nor do you need to protect the visiting preacher from receiving too much.

Most churches want two full Sundays from their evangelist. This means Sunday morning through Sunday night in a one-week revival. It is important that a visiting preacher begin a revival on Sunday morning in order to reach the morning crowd and get them back. This kind of arrangement with the following Monday-through-Saturday off means the evangelist will hold twenty-six revivals a year. Some pastors say, "I make $150 a week, so $150 for the evangelist is enough." But considering the fact that you also have house allowance, retirement, gasoline expenses, convention expenses, free secretarial help, free stationery and stamps, outside income from weddings, revivals, and funerals, $150 a week could actually total $250 a week with benefits.

A visiting evangelist, to the contrary, often must pay his own travel expenses, convention expenses, buy his own envelopes, and pay for his own retirement, health insurance, utilities, secretarial help, pictures, stationery, and so on. In the event of a prolonged sickness, he has no income. All of this should add up to an additional $50.00 a week, or $300. Multiply this by the fact that to be with you one full week means two weeks of the evangelist's time, and the result of simple arithmetic is that to live as well as the pastor, the evangelist would have to receive around $600 before any real love offering, over and above basic expenses, was given. All of these and other factors should be considered in receiving a love offering. This must be explained, publicly, to the people. Too often the people are never told that the evangelist is a full-time worker without a guaranteed income.

You should at all times be positive in the receiving of the offering. Tell the people that we have a wonderful man and it is an honor for our church to have him lead us. This is certainly not high pressure and no one will rebel at this positive approach. To the contrary, the businessmen in your church will think less of him and less of you if you pass him off as a nobody to whom they may give just anything. Never use a negative approach in the receiving of the offering. If you tell your people that this man has twenty-nine kids, a broken-down automobile, and a sick wife, they will not respond. People like to be identified with success, not misery. They will give much more if the evangelist is presented as a highly successful man whom God has blessed mightily. Neither evangelist nor pastor should ever put on the "poor act," nor should they "strut their stuff." The positive approach should always be used.

Certainly never make the mistake of telling the evangelist you will send the offering later. You like to get paid on payday—so does he. When the revival closes Sunday, payday for the visiting evangelist has arrived. Instruct the church treasurer to have the money counted, make the check, and present it immediately at the end of the services. He probably needs it then, not next week.

With your evangelist, your treasurer, your finance committee, and your people, the difference between the expense offering and love offering should be very thoroughly defined. The expenses for the special nights, publicity, travel to and from your city for the evangelist, motel, and meals should be taken from the expenses. It is best to have an amount set aside in the budget of the church to care for these expenses. If not, a special offering should be taken early in the revival with it clearly understood that it is going for the expenses of the campaign and not for the visiting singer and evangelist. This money should be put in the church treasury to help defray expenses.

After a night or two, if enough has been received for expenses, you can skip a night. If, however, at the end of two or three nights you have not received enough (no later than Wednesday night of a one-week revival, anyway), stop the expense offering. Explain to the people that if the needs have not been met, the remainder of the expenses will be cared for from the church budget. If envelopes are used for the expense offering, you should use a different kind of envelope for the love offering, beginning on Thursday night. It should be clearly stated that you are now beginning a different kind of offering and everything given from here on to the end of the campaign will go to the evangelist and singer as a love offering. It should also be clearly explained to the people what is to be done with the loose change and loose bills not given through the envelopes. Many people like to use envelopes for income-tax records. All monies given through the expense envelope should be given to the expenses and all that is loose should go for the expenses, while you are receiving expense offerings.

Everything that is given loose and through love offering envelopes should go for the love offering, while that offering is being received. Do not use the method of giving the money placed in envelopes to the love offering and the loose change to the expenses. Two distinct offerings should be taken for the two distinct purposes that you are trying to satisfy.

In the event that an evangelist is eating part or all of his meals out, he should be instructed to sign the ticket, including tip, and told that the church will take care of this. As your guest, he should be treated as such. Travel expenses to and from the meeting, unless he is going to another campaign, should be taken care of by the church. It is best to write ahead of time and see if he would prefer to have travel money sent in advance. He may need it to come to your church.

The evangelist should care for his own laundry, cleaning, long distance telephone calls, and love offering envelopes, unless the church especially wants to buy envelopes for him. It is best to use envelopes for all offerings that have checks on the back made payable to the church, it being explained that the love offering will all be given to the evangelist in one check from the church.

Love offering envelopes should not be turned over to the evangelist at the close of the campaign. He has no business building a mailing list for his personal ministry. They should be for church use only.

Occasionally, the evangelist may augment his ministry and supplement his income through the sale of books. Whether this is acceptable to the local pastor and church should be clearly understood in advance so that he will not be embarrassed by being refused after he arrives. If they are to be sold, it should be done outside of the auditorium and all money handled by the local church. The announcement concerning the sale of books should be made by the local people. This is, of course, a matter to be decided in each situation. In most churches it is entirely acceptable; in some it is not.

The actual distribution of the envelopes and the use of the offering plates to receive the offering is of tremendous importance. The most common mistake, and one of the worst, is to place offering envelopes in the plates and then pass the plates, announcing that envelopes may be obtained thereby. It is impossible for an individual to stop the offering plate, take out an envelope, fill it out, put money in it, and pass it on. *This should never be done.* People should not be asked to take the envelopes home and fill them out for the next night. There are three reasons why: (1) many of them will not be back the next night; (2) many will give every night, if the offering is taken properly, and will give much more in that way; (3) the majority of people will leave the envelope at home. Take the offering every night as though that were the only night you were going to take it. Don't mention taking it tomorrow night.

The second best way to distribute the envelopes is to put them in the pews in the envelope holders and publicly ask everyone to take one before you make the appeal for the offering. The very best way, however, is to place the envelope in the hands of the people ahead of time. This can be done at the door or by asking the ushers to come forward during the early part of the announcement time and give them out. Never ask people to raise their hands for them. You might just as well ask them to take a rattlesnake as to take an envelope. Most will not ask for one, and yet, 90 percent will give if you place an envelope in their hands. I, personally, do not like giving them at the door unless they are stapled to a bulletin or something else they are going to receive anyway. In my opinion the following method, over the years, has been the most successful and the most effortless.

At the beginning of the announcement period, ask the ushers to go to the end of each row and give ten or fifteen envelopes to the person seated on the aisle. This person will in turn pass them down his row, giving each person the opportunity to take one, whether they intend to use it or not. Tell the ushers not to say, "Do you want one?" It may be that the man on the end will refuse to jump up and down and beg for one, but that the other fifteen people on the row will want one. Extend them to the man and ask him to take one and pass them on. The extras can then be left on the seat at the other end of the row.

Do not make the appeal for the offering at this time, since you will have more announcements and special music, and much of the good of the appeal will be lost before the offering is taken. Thoroughly distribute the envelopes in this manner, asking the people to wait to fill them out until later in the service.

When the announcements are made and the last hymn has been sung, the people will stand as the ushers come forward. Remain standing as you make a good appeal, telling them of the needs, the opportunities, and the blessings of giving. Let them see you make your offering. As you fill out your envelope, they will fill out theirs. Then pray and pass the plates.

The servant is worthy of his hire. I have been on the giving and the receiving end of some very good offerings. I admonish you to remember the words of our Lord, who said, "It is more blessed to give than to receive." You cannot outgive God!

5
VISITATION

Revival week is not the time to begin cultivating prospects. It is the time to reap prospects that have been cultivated for many weeks and months. Ninety days before a recent revival, I began to cultivate fifteen couples that I felt could be reached. For five nights the evangelist and I visited in the homes of three of these couples and won twelve of them to faith in Christ. I had been in their homes, cultivating them, winning their friendship, and making them know that they could feel at home with me and that I would not pressure them. They were all converted and baptized before the revival was over.

From 5:00 P.M. to 7:00 P.M. is the best time to visit. Evening meals in the homes of members should be sacrificed for the sake of revival visitation in the early evening.

Revival time should be a time of fasting, not feasting. One meal in the homes per day is more than adequate. It is best to keep the visiting team in a motel, where they may eat in a restaurant, except for the noon meal. They will not be stuffed or feel as crowded and will be able to relax and pray. Every member of the church staff should visit during the revival and everyone in the church be asked to make one or two visits to prospects between 6:00 and 7:00 P.M.

Many of your people will be glad to eat an early supper and drop by to visit a prospect on the way to church.

Each night after the services, ask your people to remain so that you may give each of them the name of one good prospect to be contacted before the following evening services. If they are soul-winners and can lead them to faith in Christ in the homes, so much the better, but assure them that a warm and friendly invitation will also do much good. Don't scare them off by making them think they must do personal work in the homes. Assure them that their very presence will be a help, and that if they can get others to attend the services they will have done a great service.

It is always best for the pastor to visit with a layman and for another layman to go with the evangelist. As the most experienced soul-winners, the pastor and evangelist are, in that way, not wasting their time by merely listening to each other talk. If you divide up in the above manner, you will inspire and train some of your laymen and will do twice as much good on the church field.

Prospects will most likely respond during the revival if you do these things in preparing and cultivating them:

1. See them once a week for three weeks before the campaign.

2. Write them a card or letter reminding them of the revival the week before it begins.

3. Pop in on them for a minute on the Saturday night before the revival begins on Sunday. Tell them you just wanted to remind them that you'll be looking forward to seeing them tomorrow morning, and for every service possible, as your special guests.

When you go to the door to make your visit, be sure that you are dressed neatly, with breath fresh and shoes shined. Be sure that you are prayed up. Ask the Holy Spirit to prepare the heart of the person you are to visit. As you approach the door, do not talk, but walk quietly and be observant, trying to notice whether the people are in the house, in the backyard, or just what the general appearance of the situation is.

Always ring the bell rather than knocking. As the door opens, step back one step, smile, and say, "Good afternoon, may we come in?" If the family is available to talk and you are visiting people you have cultivated, you will not need to make small talk, but can begin, "Mr. Jones, I have come because I am burdened about your soul and want to see you make your decision for Christ in this revival."

I never approach the subject of conversion quickly on the first call, although I always get around to it. I use a more subtle approach. If, however, you have cultivated them with many visits and the time of reaping has arrived, come quickly to the point.

Never argue with a prospect. Always agree with his reason for believing what he does and commend him for it, if possible, but then answer him in a positive way. For example, John Doe says, "Whether I am converted or not, I can be a good man." Don't say, "No, sir, brother, you have it all wrong. You are lost and you will go to hell." Use a positive approach. "Mr. Doe, that is very commendable and I know God will help you to be a good man. We want you to see that only as you receive Jesus will you be able to be good." If he says there are hypocrites in the church, don't say, "Well, brother, I would rather be in the church with a few of them than in hell with all of them." Say, "That's right, John, there are. We are all imperfect, but Jesus will enable you to live the kind of life you desire." In other words, be respectful of the man's feelings. Give him the truth in an agreeable way. It is just as easy and much more fruitful.

If a man is won to Christ in the home, urge him to come forward that very night and make his decision public. Offer to come by and pick him up and walk forward with him. If he is saved and he has a friend in the church that has prayed for him and is interested, urge him, while you are still there, to call the friend immediately and tell him that he has just been saved. If this cannot be done, then ask the friend to call *him,* tell him that he has just heard that he has been saved, and offer to come and take him to church that night.

The value of people joining by transfer of membership should never be taken lightly. Speak to those who have shown interest, and try to have some to come each night. Their moving forward will serve as an incentive to the unsaved to come forward also.

Don't wear your evangelist out on people you know really aren't interested. Don't take him to visit your shut-ins or on hospital calls, either. Pick out two or three good prospects each night and give your time to them. You will do much more good this way than by trying to win a marathon race visiting too many people.

PROMOTION

"Pray as though it all depended on the Lord. Work as though it all depended on you." Good methods were never meant to be a substitute for prayer and the power of the Holy Spirit. Yet God will use good methods as a means of attracting people to whom we can preach after they are in attendance. Jesus used methods. He sent them out "by two and two."

Following are suggested special nights. Few of them are new—most are old—but they work. The reason they don't work sometimes is not because they are not good, but because we don't expect them to work. If you promote them with a humdrum, here-we-go-again attitude, you will get nowhere. If you will get excited and earnest about using them to enlist people to attend, your people will get excited, too.

Monday night: "Pack-a-pew Night."—You should attempt to have the largest attendance of the week on Monday. It will do much good throughout the remainder of the services of that week. If you can fill the auditorium on Monday, you can fill it every night. The best all-around attendance plan for Monday night is "Pack-a-pew."

Personally, I do not like "pew majors" and "pew generals," as there is too much breakdown of responsibility. As pastor, personally contact enough pew captains to fill the auditorium, and do it well in advance. Don't use people who already have several responsibilities during the meeting. Don't overlook the value of using your unused people here who are not normally called upon to do anything. They will likely respond beautifully to a little responsibility. A diagram of the auditorium with the number of pews and names of the captains should be placed in a prominent spot in the lobby of the church at least two weeks before the crusade begins. Privately and publicly, urge the pew captains to invite not just church members, but those who are prospects.

Tuesday night: "Junior Night."—In most revivals, a Junior service is conducted. Preach a simple message and you may have great success. If Juniors are converted on Tuesday, baptize them on Wednesday. This will bring interested parents, many of whom are themselves prospects. Don't have Junior Night late in the week, for contacts with unenlisted parents should be followed up Wednesday through Saturday.

On Sunday morning personally visit and enthusiastically tell all Juniors that there will be a hot dog supper for them one hour before the service, with games and fun. Perhaps you will want to announce a wristwatch or other award to be given to the one who brings the most other Juniors to the supper. Point out that they must stay for the service as well. Make sure that they tell their parents they are going to a religious service, not just a "hot dog supper." Have it well planned with adult workers. Start at 6:30 P.M. with supper, then have about twenty minutes for games and singing and fun. Close with a five-minute devotional and prayer, giving the Juniors time to use rest rooms and get a drink of water. Instruct the adults to take them into the auditorium and be seated with them. A card with these details should be mailed a week ahead of time to every Junior enrolled in Sunday School.

Wednesday night: "Sunday School Night."—Announce weeks ahead of time that you are asking all teachers to bring their students and sit together. Give a New Testament to all teachers who have 100 percent of their students in attendance, to the teacher of the largest class, to the oldest teacher, and to the youngest teacher.

Monday night of the revival, the evangelist should meet briefly after the service to urge upon them once again the importance of the Sunday School Night attendance plan.

Thursday night: "Youth Night."—The evangelist should announce a message of keen importance. One on morality, for example, will usually arouse much interest.

Saturday night is too late in the week to make use of the results that will usually be experienced on Youth Night. Many renewed dedications on Thursday will result in witnessing at school on Friday and the bringing of friends over the weekend. Follow the Thursday night service with a youth fellowship.

Friday night: "Guest Night."—Have a guest supper (pizza, pancake, or spaghetti) one hour before services with a prospect as the ticket of admission. Follow with music, a greeting by the pastor, and a ten-minute devotional by the evangelist. Dismiss by 7:20 P.M. and go to auditorium.

Have people introduce their guests in the evening service.

Saturday night: "Music Night."—Arrange for solos, quartets, and choir numbers in a special musical concert. The evangelist could then bring an abbreviated message and dismiss early to prepare for Sunday morning. Leave time at the close of the service for a fifteen-minute prayer meeting. Urge the people to come back for the all-night prayer service.

Morning services should be planned well in advance with ten women serving as captains to invite friends. Nurseries should be open for all services, morning and night. Ten o'clock morning services are good and sometimes a twelve o'clock noon service at a designated place in a downtown area is worthwhile. Don't have morning services just to be having them, but only if a substantial number of people can be reached.

Good promotion is a necessity. It brings people to whom you can preach the gospel of Christ. Promotion, to be effective, should be done well in advance, enthusiastically, and under the direction of the pastor. Remember the words of Jesus, "Go out into the highways and hedges, and compel them to come in, that my house may be filled." Jesus likes a full house. Use every honorable method to fill it.

7
ADVERTISING

We live in a highly modernized age. Yesterday's methods will not suffice for promoting today's product. The days of mimeographed handbills in filling stations are gone. The twentieth century demands twentieth-century methods. Let it be clearly understood that we are still promoting the oldest product in the world. It does not change, but our means of attracting people to it must. We must ever be geared to the times, but anchored to the rock when it comes to revival publicity.

Several "P's" are important in a good revival: preaching, prayer, promotion, and publicity. Advertising is merely the means by which you tell people what you have to offer them, and you will advertise your revival one way or the other. You may advertise it well, or you may advertise it poorly by failing to make it known at all; but you will give some kind of image to the world as to what you are trying to do. No advertising, a shabby presentation of the gospel, and meager crowds are certainly bad revival publicity.

First of all, be sure that you have an evangelist worthy of advertising. There are men who have the gift of preaching the evangelistic message. Get one of these men. Don't just swap pulpits with one of your friends who may or may

not be able to preach. If you do, you invite people to a
barbecue without any meat. The publicity might bring
them there the first night, but they are not likely to come
back the second. Face the fact that you need to bring a
man of outstanding preaching ability to your pulpit or the
general public is not going to be interested in hearing him
preach.

You need something special to offer. The means by which
we pipe the good news to men must be made as attractive
to the public as possible. Don't write it off as unimportant.
You will find that it is extremely important. Some men
have the gift of delivering the gospel in a more appealing
way than others. Get one of these men. Make sure that you
have something good to advertise to begin with.

Second, advertise the personality delivering the message.
Let me reemphasize, publicize the preacher. I can hear
some saying, "But we are advertising the Lord. We are
advertising new life in Christ." This is a mistake. Religious
advertising often repels rather than attracts. Don't preach
in your publicity. Build your advertising around the person
delivering the preaching. Christ said, "I, if I be lifted up
from the earth, will draw all men unto me." But if you
don't get them through the front door to hear the gospel
preached, Christ may have little opportunity to draw them.
Publicize the man delivering the message. It is the message
and the Christ that draws and saves, to be sure; but it is
through the foolishness of preaching that God has ordained
to get man in touch with the message.

Revival publicity should not be overbearing in its religious
zeal. To say, "Are you tired of sin? Try Christ. Find new

life in Jesus," is to preach to them. Don't give the plan of salvation in your publicity. God uses personalities. Advertise the preacher and the team. Then, when the people come to hear, it will be the team's job to point them to the Christ. Again, you will need to be certain that you have a man worth advertising.

Third, much free publicity can be had for the asking. Newspaper articles with fresh, interesting material about the evangelistic team and the services are always welcome at the local newspaper office and will be published free of charge. Let your article be well written and factual, with time and dates clearly stated, typed in capital letters, and double spaced. This material, along with pictures of the team, should be submitted at least two weeks before the campaign begins. A word of caution! Do not spend all your advertising dollar before the crusade begins. We often publicize too early and when the meeting begins, we have no money left. At least half (and three fourths in my opinion) of the money should be spent while the revival is in progress, and most of this in the form of newspaper advertising.

I believe the best advertisement for the money is still a newspaper ad. Television is good, but the expense is usually prohibitive. Radio is good, but don't overdo it with long announcements. A ten-second spot announcement, such as "You are invited to hear Brother Smith at the City Baptist Church, 7:30 P.M., January 19," is sufficient. Most radio stations also carry public service announcements of community events. Write them ahead of time, giving details, and they will be delighted to advertise your revival campaign.

Many radio stations have interview programs for visiting personalities. A month in advance of the revival, make arrangements with the station to have the team interviewed during their week there. If the visiting singer or preacher is an outstanding personality—perhaps a world traveler or an author—many newspapers will be delighted to arrange for a personal interview. Ask your visiting team to send pertinent information and articles from other places to you ahead of time. Take time, personally, to show this information to the religious editor, and seek to arrange an interview for the team.

Newspaper advertising must be done carefully. A few hints should be helpful.

1. Always use a picture, even a thumbnail cut of the evangelist's head, in a small ad.

2. Don't preach.

3. One column (six, eight, or ten inches) is a very good ad size—in my opinion, the best for the money.

4. Publicize special sermons to be preached on special nights if you are fairly certain that the schedule will not be changed.

5. Don't carry the pastor's picture.

6. Ask that the ad not be placed in the religious section. It will be better read elsewhere. Change the ad two or three times during the revival. Put at the top or bottom, "Five days to go," "Three days to go," "Last day," as the case may be. (A sense of urgency is always appealing.)

Fourth, handbills or window placards should be used only if you can afford to do them with one or two colors. People seldom read revival posters in black and white. Be sure to use a picture, and do not call it a revival on the window placard, but merely say, "You are invited to hear Evangelist Jones." If window cards are to be used, large cardboard posters are much better than small 8 by 11 paper handbills, and they will be better received by the merchants if distributed by adults rather than by children. Drop by immediately after the revival and offer to take down the cards and thank the merchants for displaying them. It is well, in the distributing of these cards, to take along your own thumbtacks and tape. If you really want to advertise in a big way, staple cardboard placards to small boards and distribute them to church members to be placed in front yards of homes.

A large banner, three feet by fifteen or thirty feet with bright colors, will not cost much and can be reused by changing the names and dates. These are best displayed across the main street of the town, if possible, and/or in front of the church. A sign stuck in the churchyard that merely says "Revival in Progress" is a waste of time. People do not go to hear revivals; they do go to hear John Doe preaching a revival. Advertise your revival with good publicity in front of the church.

Small printed invitations to be distributed among business associates and friends are good, but must be professionally and attractively done. In small towns it is often profitable to broadcast services live during the week. For Thursday night of the revival print a small, newspaper-type program, giving details about the progress of the revival, to be distributed by teen-agers throughout the community. Be sure to alert them not to place them in mailboxes. Attach big signs to the church bus and let it stand in different strategic spots in town the week before and the week during the revival.

Of course, the oldest way is still the very best: "Go, . . . and tell them how great things the Lord hath done for thee." Encourage your people to call their friends. It is a good idea to cut a telephone directory into sections and ask them to call everyone in their section. People should be urged to write letters and cards and call friends. Nothing is as good as an invitation from the members of your church, who are pleased that you have brought someone to their city of whom they can be proud. They will be delighted to help you advertise someone worth advertising.

PRAYER

I shall not deal at length in this book on the subject of prayer. My experiences and opinions on the subject can be read in another publication under the title *The Power of Positive Praying*.

Two brief words, however, should be given consideration. First, I do not believe there is any circumstance, any problem, any situation, that cannot result in a rich victory if the evangelist spends an hour or two or three a day on his knees in prayer. Even if no one else prays, things will happen if he does.

I have traveled across America and have never found an easy preaching situation. I have not often found a church without problems. I have seldom spent a week without excuses being made by some of the people. There is always something. It is either too hot or too cold, it is either the North or the South, the East or the West. It is always a week too early or a week too late. None of these things really matters in the slightest. Prayer, prayer, prayer is the answer. It always works; it never fails.

God will send revival and conversions if you pray. Of course, the more you can pray, the better. Obviously, the evangelist will want to join with the pastor in consistent prayer. Prayer will be the answer to every problem. For the Lord said, "If two of you shall agree on earth as touching any thing that they shall ask, it shall be done for them of my Father which is in heaven."

In my own ministry, I am never able to deceive anyone, let alone myself. When I pray, things happen in the invitation. When I don't, little happens. It is that simple.

To be sure, God sometimes blesses in answer to the prayers of others. But there are no bargain tables at God's power counter; no one can do our praying but us. No prayer, no power; little prayer, little power; much prayer, much power. There is no excuse for the evangelist not to be prayed up when he enters the pulpit. The great majority of the time his messages will be prepared well in advance of the campaign. All that is usually required of him is visitation at night, preaching the service, and praying.

Organized prayer meetings are important. Don't be discouraged, however, if only one or two come. Never berate the people for what they are not doing. Some will come late in order to make a visit before the services. Many do not come to pray because we have failed to teach them how to pray and they feel inadequate to attempt it. Others do not come and pray, simply because their hearts are cold.

Three types of prayer meetings are desirable. First is the prerevival prayer meeting. There should be at least one per week for one month prior to the revival date. Enlist all you can to attend, and make special prayer assignments. Organize cottage prayer meetings. These are simply prayer meetings of eight or ten people held in homes all over town. They should begin two weeks prior to the revival.

Organize an all-night prayer meeting for the Saturday before the revival begins and the Saturday night during the meeting. People can come to the church and pray around the clock until 8:00 A.M. the next morning. Enlist a prayer captain for each hour of the night. It will be his responsibility to enlist people to join him in prayer during his specific hour, keeping a constant chain of prayer going up to the throne of God. A blackboard should be used to add names of those for whom people request prayer. Let the hourly prayer leaders be the deacons and leaders of the church. Quote Jeremiah 33:3 and 2 Chronicles 7:14 and other appropriate prayer verses throughout the night.

The evangelist or pastor should lead nightly prayer meetings before the regular services. Perhaps the evangelist could lead an adult prayer meeting and the pastor a prayer meeting for teen-agers and children. Let them make their requests and pray around in a circle after the leader begins. He should close the prayer meeting five minutes prior to the services.

Organized prayer meetings need to be announced and promoted. Publicize and push them and people will pray and the power will fall and people will come. If you don't, it will not and they won't!